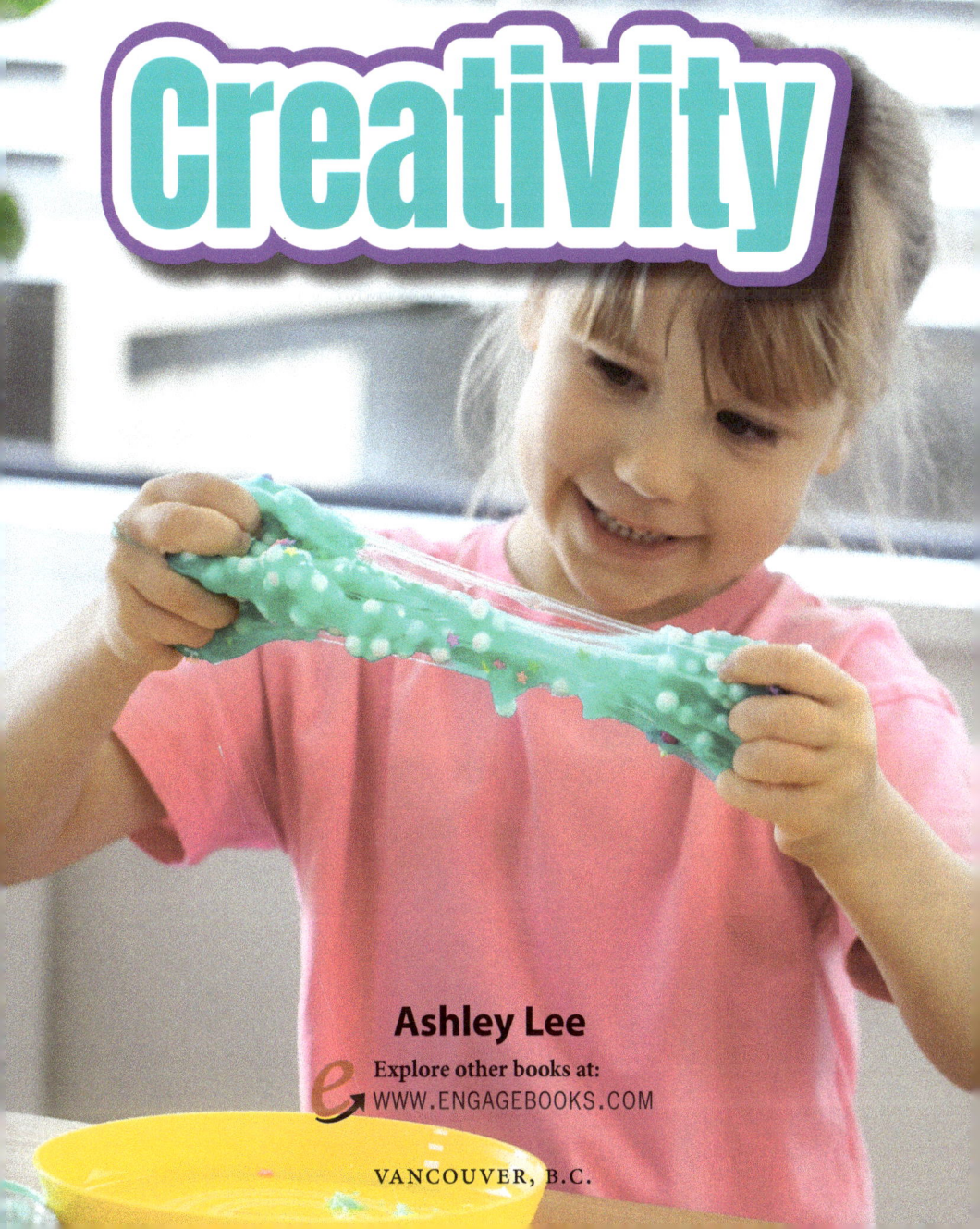

# Good Character Traits

# Creativity

## Ashley Lee

Explore other books at:
WWW.ENGAGEBOOKS.COM

VANCOUVER, B.C.

**WWW.ENGAGEBOOKS.COM**

*Creativity: Good Character Traits*
Lee, Ashley, 1995 –
Text © 2025 Engage Books
Design © 2025 Engage Books

Edited by: A.R. Roumanis
Design by: Mandy Christiansen

Text set in Myriad Pro Regular.
Chapter headings set in Anton.

FIRST EDITION / FIRST PRINTING

LIBRARY AND ARCHIVES CANADA CATALOGUING IN PUBLICATION

Title: Creativity / Ashley Lee.
Names: Lee, Ashley, author.
Description: Series statement: Good Character Traits

ISBN 978-1-77878-723-2 (hardcover)
ISBN 978-1-77878-729-4 (softcover)

This project has been made possible in part
by the Government of Canada.

Canada

# Creativity

# Contents

4  What Is Creativity?

6  Why Is Creativity Important?

8  What Does Creativity Look Like?

10  How Does Creativity Affect You?

12  How Does Creativity Affect Others?

14  Is Everyone Creative?

16  Is It Bad if You Are Not Creative?

18  Does Creativity Change Over Time?

20  Is It Hard to Be Creative?

22  How Can You Learn to Be More Creative?

24  How Can You Help Others Be More Creative?

26  How to Be Creative Every Day

28  Creativity Around the World

30  Quiz

# What Is Creativity?

Creativity means using your **imagination** to think of new ideas.

Creativity comes from being able to look at things in a new way.

It takes creativity to look at a cloud and see a dog or happy face.

# Why Is Creativity Important?

Creativity helps people have fun and create new things.

It helps people find ways to deal with their problems.

# What Does Creativity Look Like?

There are many different ways of being creative. Some people paint or draw pictures.

Other people write stories or create new **inventions**.

**Key Word**

**Inventions:** new things that people have made.

# How Does Creativity Affect You?

Being creative makes you feel happy and **proud**.

## Key Word

**Proud:** feeling good because of something you have done.

It can also help make your **mental health** better.

**Key Word**

**Mental health:** the health of your mind.

# How Does Creativity Affect Others?

Creativity can help people understand each other.

It can help people share
their thoughts and feelings.

# Is Everyone Creative?

Some people are more creative than others. But everyone can be creative.

**Practice** can help you become more creative.

## Key Word

**Practice:** do something over and over again to get better at it.

Kids are often more creative than adults.

# Is It Bad if You Are Not Creative?

It is not bad if you are not creative. Everybody is good at different things.

But most
people are
creative even
if they do
not know it.

# Does Creativity Change Over Time?

Some people get less creative as they get older.

Other people use their creativity to do something they love when they get older.

# Is It Hard to Be Creative?

Being creative is easy for some people. They can be creative without even trying.

Other people need to work hard at being creative.

# How Can You Learn to Be More Creative?

Spend time with creative people. You can learn a lot from them.

Try new things and do not be afraid to make mistakes.

Creativity helps people fix mistakes.

# How Can You Help Others Be More Creative?

Do something creative together. Play games or paint a picture.

Listen to other people's ideas. Do not say mean things about their ideas.

# How to Be Creative Every Day

1. Take time to **daydream.**

2. Create something new like a picture or a story.

3. Ask "what if" questions.

4. Play lots of games.

## Key Word

**Daydream:** when you get lost in your thoughts and forget about what you are doing.

# Creativity Around the World

Every part of the world shows creativity in different ways.

They all have their own ways of creating art and music.

# Quiz

Test your knowledge of creativity by answering the following questions. The questions are based on what you have read in this book. The answers are listed on the bottom of the next page.

**1** Does creativity help people find ways to deal with their problems?

**2** Are there many different ways of being creative?

**3** Can creativity help make your mental health better?

**4** Can everyone be creative?

**5** Is it bad if you are not creative?

**6** Do some people need to work hard at being creative?

# Explore Other Level 1 Readers.

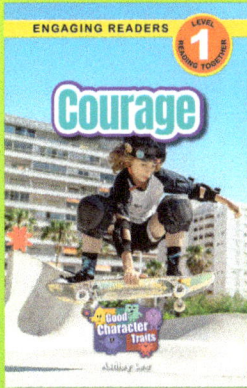

Courage

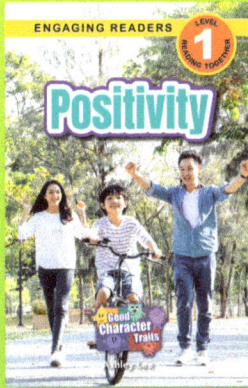

Positivity

Resilience

Respect

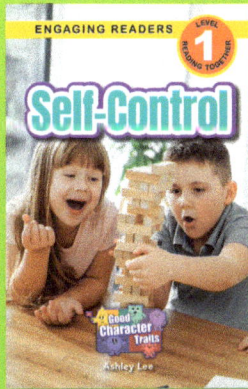

Self-Control

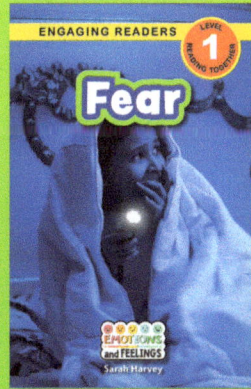

Fear

Happiness

Sadness

Surprise

Visit www.engagebooks.com/readers

www.ingramcontent.com/pod-product-compliance
Lightning Source LLC
Chambersburg PA
CBHW052035030426
42337CB00027B/5014